MW00479963

MEDITATION MANUAL

Simple Directions To

A Life-Changing Practice

Peggy Ludington

ISBN: 978-1-09839-767-8 (Paperback)
ISBN: 978-1-09839-768-5 (eBook)

Book cover design by nskvsky

Published courtesy of Ludington Institute For Family Enrichment

For my husband Alan,
whose unwavering love
set my heart free.

"The greatest revelation is stillness."

– Lao Tsu

Preface

This book is a bite-size guide to help you *immediately* begin meditating (or enhance your meditation practice). Easy to read in twenty to thirty minutes, it's not like other meditation books. Those are typically two hundred to three hundred pages explaining various traditions, philosophies, techniques, and scientific data—great for understanding meditation and why it works.

This is not that.

Whether you are new to meditation, looking to begin again, a current meditation app user wishing for something more, or a seasoned meditator wanting a fresh experience, this little book can help you awaken to a level of awareness you may not have known is possible.

Author's Note

My Winding Road To Meditation . . .

When I was seventeen, Richard Bach, author of then-new *Jonathan Livingston Seagull*, spoke to my high school humanities class. He and my favorite teacher, Sarah Jane Carty, were transcendental meditation friends. Though he wasn't pitching meditation, there was something about his energy, his presence, that captivated me.

That night, I asked my parents for permission to learn transcendental meditation. At the time, meditation was new to the United States. Mainstream considered it part of the counter culture and drug scene, maybe even a cult. Understandably, my parents said, "No." The seed of interest went dormant.

I attended Pepperdine University, studied abroad, and went on to UCLA Law School. Adult life looked promising until my first day as law clerk for the elected county prosecutor.

That day my father—a criminal defense lawyer and my mentor—was snagged by an overly broad DEA dragnet in the largest drug importation scheme of its time. A very long story. Suffice to say, watching him falsely accused and railroaded through two absurd trials derailed my love for the law.

Two years later, my mother, my sister, and I were visiting him at the federal penitentiary. It was Christmas Eve. In the fog-filled visitors' yard, my sister innocently asked, "Dad, how did this happen to you?"

Time froze. I had sheltered her from so much of the ordeal. Now, here she was asking.

"It was my idea," he confessed, almost boastfully. "All of it."

Wait, what?

At first, I thought he was kidding. He was not. I'd given up a year and a half of my life trying to save him from this miscarriage of justice and failed, or so I'd thought. The shock of it sent me on a nine-month emotional freefall that landed me in therapy.

Six months in, my psychologist—a lifelong meditator and yogi—suggested that both meditation and yoga would help me with my depression and anxiety. I didn't bite. Yoga was too slow for a runner and gym rat like me, and I was too busy for meditation.

Eventually, my life reconstituted. I fell in love, married, sold my law practice, and raised two amazing sons (the most rewarding thing I've ever done). *Then*, they grew up and left for college.

I felt suddenly lost. My motherhood sails lay in tatters. I had no purpose. Another crash-and-burn moment for my spirit.

While therapy had dug me out of my first crash, it would be meditation that saved me from this one.

I was turning fifty when an older, wiser friend, Jacqueline Henderson, gifted me a day at sweat lodge. She explained that age fifty was a "year of transformation." I *really* did not want this gift. Trepidation and anxiety filled me in the weeks leading up to it, but no way could I say, "Thanks, but no thanks," not to her.

Turns out trepidation may be the doorway to transformation. Sweat lodge was grueling, and hot, and unfamiliar. Everyone was clothed, thank goodness. The physical and emotional struggle of it, facing (and surviving) my fears, led me to yoga. Yoga opened me to meditation.

But how to learn?

This was long before the proliferation of meditation apps. I listened to recordings by gurus, attended seminars, and read so many books, all in pursuit of the elusive "right way." I learned solid tradition, technique, and philosophy. Yet, I struggled. I just felt like I was sitting with my eyes closed, focusing on my breath (or mantra), while on the lookout for my "thinking mind."

Was this the entire experience?

Then, I met my friend, Christine Lang, a medical intuitive and fellow lawyer. She assured me there was no "right way" to meditate. She taught me some of her techniques (several of which I include here because I still use them). Her guidance freed me to cobble together my own path, one that worked for me. I wish the same for you.

If this method works for you, please use it, use *any part* of it. If not, please keep searching. My hope is you won't stop until you find your own path to the peace, comfort, and awareness that meditation provides.

Much love,

Peggy

www.peggyludington.com

Introduction
To Meditation

A Bit About Meditation . . .

Meditation allows us to become acquainted with the separation between the Brain, the Mind and our Essence.

The Brain is an organ—the body's computer. It filters every sight, touch, taste, scent, sound, and sensation that we *choose* to perceive. It telegraphs information to other parts of the body, and to the Mind.

The Mind, as I think of it, is our intelligence, our discernment. It tells us about the sensory stimuli filtering through the Brain. "That's hot." "That's bitter." "That's beautiful." "That's loud." It also provides a running monologue narration of our lives, chattering endlessly, sometimes judgmentally. "Boy, can she be annoying." "Turn left here." "I think I'd like an ice cream."

The Brain perceives raw data, aka *neutral reality.* The Mind then *colors, sorts, catalogues, and judges* it according to our life's training and previously stored experiences.

The Mind is very good at judging and comparing, and an amazing squirrel hole for *Jeopardy* and *Trivial Pursuit* answers. It is our Courtroom of Opinion, whereas the Brain is our Temple of Observation.

The Brain perceives the approach of a speeding car, which triggers a chemical alert in the body. The Mind assesses, and the narration begins: "Oh my god—That car might hit me!"

A nanosecond later, a voice/thought wells up from the quiet center that exists deep inside each of us: "Stay calm. Move quickly."

We've all experienced finding inner strength in the face of immense challenge or loss, knowing something in our "heart of hearts," or discovering a solution to a tangled problem at the most unexpected moment. But where do inner strength, deep knowing, and creative inspiration come from? They aren't qualities you can tap into by thinking about them. None is really a process of conscious thought. Rather, they are produced by some other aspect of our being. They *come to us*, often subtly like dawn breaking. But, from where? Meditation opens the door to understanding the answer.

Inside each of us is a wellspring of wisdom and truth. It is the source of all intuition, inner strength, inspiration, and deep knowing. I call this place our Essence. Meditation provides access to it.

Meditation can have a profound effect on our lives without being a profound experience. Don't worry if you feel like you're not "getting it," not doing it "right." Your goal isn't ethereal transcendence. It is simple stillness. Our minds are always "on" with inner dialog and problem-solving. Our goal is to step outside this "thinking" and out of the logical mind, even for a moment.

Meditation is simply a quieting of the mind and body that allows us to connect with our deepest Essence—our truest being.

We call meditation a *practice* for a reason. You're never perfect at it. But by committing to the practice, your mind begins to quiet. You begin to reap the benefits. You'll notice decreased anxiety, a sense of calm and ease, a broader perspective about your life, an increased capacity for relaxation, as well as enhanced mental clarity, agility, and focus—and you'll soon notice you have the choice to *respond* rather than react.

For those who've never tried meditation, there might be a fear of "losing control," as if in a meditative state you may do something you don't want to do. Meditation isn't like that. It's not magic, it's not religious, it's not cosmic woo-woo stuff. It's merely focused attention—stillness. You're awake, alert, and aware the entire time. You can stop at any time.

What follows is my method of reaching the meditative state, a place of connection with deep awareness. It is the way I journey inward, the path that I take. There is no "right way" to meditate. This method is but one pathway, one woven together from the teachings of many teachers. *Use only what resonates with you.*

Meditation should be user-friendly. It shouldn't be hard, or grueling, or boring. At the very least, it should be an enjoyable break.

Because I'm a visual learner, mine is a visual path. I will provide you with a series of images, like scenes in a movie. Let yourself experience them, actually inhabit them. Each image is a stepping stone on the pathway.

The meditation instructions that follow contain four exercises that build on each other:

Exercise 1—Ocean Breathing

Exercise 2—Setting Your Channel

Exercise 3—Raising Your Energy and Quieting Your Thoughts

Exercise 4—The Journey

The first three exercises prepare your body and mind for meditation. Each is a freestanding technique to achieve relaxation, focus, and awareness. They're like mini meditations. Once you know them, you can travel through all three rapidly in a matter of a minute or two. Or you may choose to linger on each step—it's lovely to feel your body and mind become calm and alert.

When you move on to Exercise 4, you will begin with the first three techniques to prepare yourself. They will help you settle and center. They build the foundation for the meditation experience of Exercise 4.

Exercise 4, The Journey, is a guided passage to the meditative state and connection with deep awareness. Don't worry if it takes a bit of time to reach stillness in your first sessions. Once you internalize the visual and auditory cues, you will reach it more quickly.

However, even after you know your pathway, there will be occasions when you feel yourself struggling to "get there"—at least that happens to me. Just slow down. Focus on each step again like you did when you were learning. Remember: It's a *practice*.

MEDITATION INSTRUCTIONS

THE SEATED POSTURE

Maintaining an upright posture (if it's possible for you) enables you to raise your energy toward the crown of your head. It supports being alert and awake.

Sit comfortably on the floor, or in a chair. If you're in a chair, let your feet rest flat on the floor, or sit yoga style (crossed-legged with your feet on the chair, too). If you're on the floor, yoga style is best, but you may want some height under your tailbone (like a cushion, pillow, or folded blanket), so you can easily retain the normal curve of your spine.

Set your head in easy balance atop this curve.

Let your upturned hands rest comfortably on your thighs.

Accept the support of Earth beneath you.

Now, let's begin . . . The Breath—You are the ocean.

EXERCISE 1:

THE BREATH

Ocean Breathing

This technique will allow you to relax and sharpen your focus.

Close your eyes.

Become aware of your breath. Inhale slowly for the count of four or five. Exhale for the same count. Establish an easy rhythm.

Let your shoulders drop. Relax your heart. Unclench your stomach.

As your breathing becomes comfortable, imagine watching a gentle surf glide in and out across a smooth sandy shore. In and out. Match your breath to its rhythm.

Without changing the rhythm, *become the ocean*. As the wave rejoins the sea, gently gather your breath back into you. Then, release it softly onto the sand with your exhale.

Your spent wave of breath naturally returns as you inhale. Exhale and watch the frothy lace spread across the sand and stretch to its limit.

Feel the breath wave roll back into you, refilling your lungs. Release another, noting the soft hiss as the water fills tiny spaces in the sun-warmed sand.

At its farthest reach, the exhaled wave *pauses*, then slides back into you, tumbling small shells and pebbles. Once the breath rejoins you, it *pauses*. Release it again.

Enjoy the slow, rolling rhythm of the breath wave. Become aware of the pauses where the water changes course—the space between inhales and exhales. Continue for several rounds.

Now, focus on the *sound* of your breath. Let it reflect the sound of the ocean as it gathers and releases. On your next exhale, through parted lips, whisper: "Ahhh" (like a relaxing sigh). On your inhale, let the slow intake of air through your mouth create another whispered "Ahhh." (Notice a *slight expansion* at the back of throat as the air passes through.) Repeat for several rounds.

On your next exhaled "Ahhh," halfway through, gently close your lips and maintain the sound through your nose. (Feel the *very slight constriction* of the nasal airway as it creates this quiet sound.) Slowly inhale through your nose, creating an "Ahhh" as the breath wave returns to you. (A *soft expansion* of your nasal airway while inhaling helps create this.)

Continue this *very soft, slumber-like sound,* with its rolling rhythm, until you feel deeply relaxed.

Your breath now mirrors the sound of a gentle surf.

You are the ocean.

A NOTE:

Breathing in this way dramatically soothes your nervous system. It reassures your body that its standby mode of flight-fight-freeze is unneeded.

You can use Ocean Breathing anytime to relax or get a grip. It's also the first step in preparing yourself to meditate. As you move on to the other exercises, start with Ocean Breathing (lips closed) until you feel fully relaxed. Then begin the exercise and allow the breath to breathe itself. You don't need think about it anymore. If, at any time, you feel distracted or wish to go deeper, do a couple rounds of Ocean Breathing. The sound alone will deepen your relaxation and focus.

EXERCISE 2:

SETTING YOUR CHANNEL

Root, Earth, and Sky

Through this exercise, you'll further prepare yourself for the meditative state of deep awareness. First, we visualize creating an energy channel within the body. Almost like choosing a channel so you can watch or listen to a certain station, you are dialing in your body and mind to a quiet frequency. This may seem a bit odd at first. I know how strange it felt to me when I was learning. Just give it a try. It helps open you for meditation.

Close your eyes.

Begin Ocean Breathing until you feel settled.

Now, focus your awareness on the center of your brow. You may see the shape of an eye or feel as if you're looking into the eye of another.

Hear the words: "I Am Here." Allow them to dissolve through your brow center and slide down your spine into Earth, sending down a root all the way to Earth's core.

With this root connection established, feel Earth energy entering the soles of your feet, traveling up the back of your legs to the base of your spine.

At the same time, feel Sky energy entering through your crown. Let it travel down the *back* of your spine to your base, where it meets and mixes with small bits of Earth energy. (Any excess Earth energy can be easily discharged back into Earth through that deep root you've set.)

Draw this blended energy up the *front* of your spine, through the seven energy centers located there, raising it slowly until you feel it fill each one:

1. First, it fills and spins at the *base of your spine.*

2. It moves up to fill and spin at the *midline between your hips.*

3. Now, up to your *solar plexus*, below the diaphragm and above the navel.

4. Then, up to your *heart space*—it expands and fills your chest, flowing into your arms.

5. Up to the notch in your *throat*, where your voice resides.

6. Next, to your *brow center*, site of your wisdom and vision.

7. And at last, it flows out the *crown of your head* and through your upturned palms, like a golden fountain.

A NOTE:

You now are deeply rooted in the Earth. You feel Earth-Sky energy flowing through you, clearing the cobwebs and blockages. Your channel is open and receptive.

EXERCISE 3:

RAISING YOUR ENERGY

AND

QUIETING YOUR THOUGHTS

Your energy channel is clearest when your energy is gathered, condensed, and then raised above your head, like an antenna for the meditation frequency. We intensify the power of that "antenna" by reclaiming the energy that we all scatter while attending to our hectic lives.

RAISING YOUR ENERGY

Close your eyes.

Begin Ocean Breathing until relaxed.

Focus on your brow center. Feel the words "I Am Here" dissolve into you, growing your root deep into Earth.

Allow Earth-Sky energy to clear your channel as it flows into you and out your crown and palms.

Next, let's reclaim and settle your busy energy. At your center, imagine a magnetic beam of light. It attracts all the energy you hold internally, as well as the energy you send out to handle your busy life. Your scattered energy can't resist its pull. Feel the fragments returning to you.

Once your energy has collected in that beam, compress it like a snowball, a snowball of the purest white light.

In your mind's eye, watch that energy ball float up and out your crown, where it hovers just above your head, a radiant orb of snow-white light. This is where your energy will remain during meditation. If you'd like, help it stay lifted by visualizing it in a shallow vessel above your crown.

QUIETING YOUR THOUGHTS

Now, it's time to quiet the chattering mind.

See yourself climbing the porch steps of an old-fashion farmhouse. You enter and climb two flights of stairs until you reach its spacious wooden attic—the kind kids love to play in.

Above its well-loved belongings, you see beautiful floating balloons with lustrous satin ribbons of every color. They bump softly against the ceiling and rafters. You realize these are your thoughts, bumping around inside your head.

Walk through the attic, gathering up the ribbons with their attached thought balloons. Check every nook.

Once you've gathered them all, open the large shuttered window. Gently press the balloons out the window and release them to the breeze. Watch their ribbons twirl as they disappear into the clear blue sky.

A NOTE:

Your mind should feel quiet now. If you become aware of a returning thought, you can release it as a balloon or place it in a bubble and softly brush it aside.

Be gentle with your thoughts. Try not to judge yourself for having them, or for dancing with them. That is the nature of the mind. When you notice you're engaged with one, simply realize it's your mind "thinking" again and release it.

EXERCISE 4:

THE JOURNEY

The Cave, The Cove, The Cosmos

Now that you've learned how to set your channel, raise your energy, and quiet your mind, we can begin the journey to the meditative state.

Close your eyes.

Begin Ocean Breathing until relaxed.

Focus on your brow center. Feel the words "I Am Here" dissolve into you as you send your root deep into Earth.

Allow Earth-Sky energy to clear your channel as it flows into you and out your crown and palms.

Take a moment to reclaim your energy. Raise it above your crown.

Walk through the attic gathering your thought balloons. Release them to the breeze.

You are ready. Let's turn inward and dive into your depths.

Imagine yourself swimming through your inner being. It's like an underwater sea cave, cool and a bit dim. Up ahead, there's light at your center. Swim to it.

Once there, you find a column of bright water filled with tiny bubbles rising upward. Swim into the bright water. Allow yourself to rise on its effervescence.

Up above, you see the glimmer of the surface as it grows closer.

When your face breaks the surface of the water, you breathe deeply. You discover you're in a beautiful sun-drenched cove. The water temperature, the air temperature— they're perfect.

You taste the salt on your lips as you begin to swim through the warm water toward the nearby sandy shore. Notice how strong your body feels swimming, the flutter of your kick, the pull of your arms. You feel vital and alive.

When you can, stand and walk to the edge of the wet sand. Feel every grain as your feet press into it. Once at the water line, sit down and face the sea.

Take in the exquisite beauty here. You are nourished by it. You feel energy all around you. The soft lapping waves echo your own calm, rhythmic breathing. You feel deeply grateful to be in this place.

Notice the total absence of shadows in this cove. There is no single source of light. Instead, everything glows from within. Even the air particles have a golden twinkle.

This is a magical, peaceful cove. You feel good that you know the way here and that you can come back anytime.

Looking around from your seat on the warm sand, your eyes travel the tree-dotted shoreline to your right. Once they reach the point, take your awareness there.

At the point, the first thing you notice is a billowy column of "clouds" that reaches into the sky. It is a nebula, illuminated by the radiant colors of sunset and dawn. Marigold. Peach. Rose. You feel energy rising through its center.

Allow yourself to be drawn up and into its energy funnel, surrounded by the colorful billows. You feel childlike joy. The colors caress you as you rise.

Gazing upward, you feel a sense of lift emitting from your face and chest. Ahead, you see an opening. Rise toward it. Near the upper edge of the nebula, the colors shift. Aqua. Periwinkle. Violet.

You emerge through the opening. You are floating in the stillness of space surrounded by millions of stars.

Lie back. Relax into the support it gives you. Your limbs spread gently, as if to reach in all directions. You float here like a five-pointed star.

A tranquil sea of energy supports you. You are floating on the surface of pure Awareness.

Everywhere you look is infinity. Time stretches to eternity in all directions. This stillness—this quiet—is Source. Light is *everywhere* even though it looks dark between the stars.

This is an expansive place. You feel yourself expanding to meet it. You are one with it. Absorb its peace. Feel its tranquility. You are safe. You are loved. You feel home.

You have entered deep meditation.

Here you can tune in to truth, wisdom, knowing, all facets of your deepest Essence. Feelings, images, words, ideas, and sounds may gently drift into you. Treat them as messages of this realm.

You can float a question into this space. Wait for a response with patience. It may take practice to perceive it. You also may find you can ask your awareness to transport you to different places and perspectives (like it did when it took you to the cove's point without walking).

Or simply float here and enjoy the peace and serenity that surround you.

A NOTE:

As a goal, build up your meditation time to twenty minutes or more. However, even as little as five minutes will yield benefits.

Because of the floating, suspended sensation of deep meditation, it's helpful to consciously recenter and reground yourself before ending your session. To do this, follow the next method.

THE RETURN

When ready, before opening your eyes, use this process for stepping back down and back into your life:

Become aware of your breath.

Feel yourself floating back down into your body.

Know that your experience on this journey is now part of you.

Become aware of your surroundings.

Reinhabit your body. Move your fingers and toes.

Feel Earth supporting you.

Center your awareness behind your eyes.

Swallow.

When you feel ready, open your eyes.

You are back.

A NOTE:

As you develop your personal meditation practice, you may wish to begin with some little ritual—perhaps lighting a candle, playing meditation music, or reading something that speaks to your heart. Contemplative or inspirational writings and poetry work well. (My practice begins with lighting a candle and reading aloud a passage from Mark Nepo's The Book of Awakening.*)*

As you close your practice, another small ritual is nice. It will help you reground. Some possibilities might be: Take a moment to experience and express gratitude. Recite a positive affirmation or prayer. Choose a quality you wish to embody throughout your day (like compassion, patience, kindness, joy) and set your intention to do so. Your ending ritual also can be something as simple as a sip of water. Find whatever works best for you.

A Parting Note

Thank you for reading my little book and for joining me on this journey. I hope it offered you a glimpse of your true nature, and a momentary break from the incessant chatter of the busy mind. That alone can be worth the price of admission.

As you begin your own meditation practice, please allow yourself to modify these instructions in any way that best suits you. Maybe you don't like balloons—so substitute a flock of doves roosting in the attic rafters. It's your practice. You get to design it. Create your own path.

By the way, if an audio version of these exercises would be helpful for you as you internalize your path, please visit my website peggyludington.com for links.

I wish you well. May you always live your life as a seeker, blessed with childlike wonder and excited to see what lies around the next bend.

Namaste.

Peggy

Acknowledgements

With Much Gratitude . . .

This book is the product of a lifetime of seeking, and the love and encouragement of some very important people.

First, my husband Alan, who is always my number one fan, no matter what direction life takes me (there have been many). His belief in me is the wind on which I've soared for thirty-five years.

Our children, Logan, Trevor, and Liz, whose love and joy give me great purpose and the greatest gratification. What a gift it is to share life with them.

My sister, Pattie Brunner, who sifts through words and ideas with such a keen mind. Her input was perspective-giving and seminal. My lifelong sister-friend, Cyndi Coombes, whose pride makes me feel like I've won the blue ribbon.

I am ever grateful to my teacher, Sarah Jane Carty, and her friend Richard Bach for planting the seed of curiosity in me and for my utter acceptance that *meditation makes life sweeter.*

To Jackie Henderson, my friend and personal guru, who watered that seed until it finally sprouted. To Christine Lang, another dear friend, for urging me to discover my own pathway to meditation, and for teaching me a number of this pathway's components. And, to Delfina Alden, a very special person in my life, without whose urging this manual simply would not exist.

This writing ultimately came together because of the thoughtful input of treasured friends who read early versions. To Kate Crump, Debbie Martin, Sandy Jacobs, Alan Rich, Pamela Fong Rich, and Melody Black— their encouragement made me braver, their clear and insightful suggestions made this manual stronger.

Thank you all.